Release Me

50 Modern Poems

Jean-Claude Agomate

Copyright © 2019 Jean-Claude Agomate

All rights reserved. No part of this book may be reproduced or transmitted in any form or by any means, electronic or mechanical, including photocopying, recording or by an information storage and retrieval system – except by a reviewer who may quote brief passages in a review to be printed in a magazine, newspaper or on the Web – without permission in writing from the author.

Published in the United States by LeParadigm Books, Virginia
www.leparadigmbooks.com

Cover design by Harper Skye Designs

For no one and everyone

ENJOY THE RIDE

There can be no life, but by death…death of the belief that one is incapable of aspiring toward and achieving that which is greater than oneself. The duality of man and destiny of one who believes in the power of belief are bound by the twine of totality. Totality in lieu of fate may be possible to the extent that one does not believe in fate. If one believes in fate, then totality can never be attained, as the person in question is not in control, but merely along for the ride.

Jean-Claude Agomate

CONTENTS

A HOOT 1
AFICIONADO 2
BAD PENNY 3
BIRD SONG 4
BUCKET LIST 5
BUG GIRL 6
BY THE WAY 7
CHILD 8
CHOICES 9
DENIED LOVE 10
DONUT AND COFFEE 11
DRAGON 12
EGGS AND HAMMY 13
FAREWELL 14
FORGING STEEL 15
GIVE ME YOUR HAND 16
GRATEFUL 17
GREAT SONG 18
HOW TO LOSE 19
IMMORTALITY 20
INSIGNIFICANT 21
KETCHUP 22
LEARNING AND UNDERSTANDING 23
LEFT AND RIGHT 25
LOVE ME NOT 26
MANIFESTATION OF LOVE 27
MANKIND 28
MARRIAGE 30
MEMORY 31
MESSAGE IN A BOTTLE 32

MUSTARD	33
NATIVE REVERENCE	34
ONE PERCENT	35
ONE WISH	36
PARENTS	37
PONDER	38
PURPLE SADNESS	39
RAINBOW (ODE TO SUSAN)	40
REJECT	42
RUN RUN RUN	43
SAD HORSE	44
SIDES OF A COIN	45
TAKE MY BODY HOME	46
THE END	47
THE MOON AND BEYOND	48
THE WORLD IS NOT BIG ENOUGH	49
TIME MACHINE	50
TWIST	51
WHEN I'M OLD	52
WHERE YOU STAND	53

A HOOT

If I were to say hoot, would you think of an owl
Or a rabbit at a renaissance racing from scowls
Of people whose raison d'être compels them to growl
Like animals at animals sans beastly howls
A hoot is a term that's given to strange
Like she's an odd duck, socially shortchanged
Like he's a poor schmuck, soon to be estranged
From no one that is someone to a man deranged
A hoot takes its root from the act of humor
If you don't get it, then you might be the humor
A human that is humorous, but fails to see
In thy very presence, spake they not unto thee
But about thee in a round about way
You didn't ask for life, why should you have to pay
For errors in your parents' judgment, bringing you forth
Into a world of twisted judgment, no true north
Imagine for a tick that hoots were not sound
Nor folks to make fun of on meaningless grounds
If hoots were mythical and magical in presence
With feet so massive that they were excrescence
Imagine for a tick that I had a real hoot
I'd journey to Canada and ask them aboot
A boot for a hoot that is rare to hoots
The correct term is aboat, so they can't venture aboot
Unless through your mind, if you're able to give pause
To the silliness of wonderment, to serve a child's cause
To accept the world with its flaws and not refute
For at the end of the day, who really gives a hoot

AFICIONADO

Aficionado and bravado shared a bottle of scotch
It was pored by insanity as reason watched
It affected humanity by shaving time off the clock
How vain is our vanity, never seeing the plot
Aficionado and bravado hatched an evil plan
They would patter to the left, obscuring the right hand
A hand that understands what it means to cheat life
Or give it, as it is told, bringing chaos to life
Aficionado and bravado planned to rule the world
They drifted and sifted through flags to unfurl
A flag that's a gag, as it's a means to an end
A patriot that's false may lead to one's end
Aficionado and bravado are clearly in league
A war not of words, but invisible blitzkriegs
You may call it absurd, blame foreboding fatigue
But death becomes those who lack intrigue

BAD PENNY

Mountains may crumble and sea levels may rise
You can't get rid of me; I'm like a bad penny
The end of the earth is but certain we surmise
You can't get rid of me; I'm like a bad penny
Famine and drought as the rich compromise
You can't get rid of me; I'm like a bad penny
When money is worthless there's no compromise
You can't get rid of me; I'm like a bad penny
Riots and shooting and looting take hold
You can't get rid of me; I'm like a bad penny
Pray for the young as you care for the old
You can't get rid of me; I'm like a bad penny
Lava, pollution, and ice in the fold
You can't get rid of me; I'm like a bad penny
Humanity extinct, as she cleanses the mold
I got rid of you, now I'm simply a penny

BIRD SONG

If I were a bird, I would fall from the sky
I would simply stop flapping and close my bird eyes
Cloud after cloud, I would swiftly fall through
Ten seconds to live, oh what should I do
I've led and I've followed in flight and for soar
God made me bird, perhaps there is more
More to consider, contemplation so new
Six seconds left, oh what shall I do
I think of my mother, she taught me bird song
My vision gets blurry as I sing my bird song
My breathing is shallow…my heart starts to pound
Three seconds left before I hit the ground
A bird in a sky full of birds, no big loss
A bird about to die, not a soul to mourn the loss
As sad as it is, I'm about to gain release
In an instant it's over, no more seconds, just peace

BUCKET LIST

My bucket list is full of things that make me wonder why
I'd place them on a to-do list as if I'm gonna die
I'll live to be a thousand years before I close the door
To the current world I know, then live a thousand more
I want to jump from planes above and dive into the air
And twist and fold and hurl and mold my body like I care
But do I care enough to heed instructors' sane advice
And pull my chute before I die, perhaps that's sage advice
A twinkle of a trebuchet before it fires hot
Is what I feel, life's highlight reel, oh my, how I forgot
My bucket list is quite amiss, as items there are strange
Like dressing like a clown with shaped balloons, am I deranged
Perhaps, my head is mostly lead with only three brain cells
I wonder how I function, Lord, at times I want to yell
But yell, I may and yell, I might, no sound just pain entrenched
A cell of clay, a futile plight, a scarecrow in a trench
My bucket list is full of things that make me wonder why
I'd place them on a to-do list, I'm never gonna die
I'll live to be a million years before I close the door
To the current world I know, then live a million more
I want to learn Italian, Japanese, and lovely Greek
And sign with my hands, not a word, yet I speak
Communication, many nations, built to be so strong
Yet, greed overtakes the pure, as sure as time is long
A diatribe for many tribes that argue over land
Religion and superiority, slight of hand
A hand of light, a light of love, has taught me not to dwell
On that with which I cannot change, wolf tickets do not sell
As such, we all should think of things that we would like to do
And add them to a bucket list, which represents us true
Sixty years or thirty more, longevity is strife
What matters is not mortality, but how you live your life

BUG GIRL

The strangest of things becomes those that aid
High wires of worth, to cross is forbade
Like morals of stories, their gore and their glory
Spared by the bus, but hit by the lorry
The goodness of fear and danger combined
The concept of life and death intertwined
The tracks of a train with bolts ye are loose
A fork in that turkey, a smile for that goose
A parachute opened with holes all about
Like eating ice-cream with bugs in your mouth
Crunch, oh you must, for ground or for bug
Yuck, still alive, I'm sorry, no hug
I'd help, but good deeds are punished you see
I feed one kitty cat, tomorrow there're three
Oh shucks, I'll do it, I'll help you bug girl
With a mouth full of bugs, you and I will change the world

BY THE WAY

By the way, have I told you how special you are
How reason hath reason to distance so far
From anything special that is other than you
For you are the light that defines the moon
A moon that's not great without those who behold
A match without sulfur, a blizzard without cold
How bland life would be without someone so true
At risk of cliché, there's no me without you
By the way, have I told you how terrible you are
How reason hath reason to not distance far
From everything special that is other than you
Your logic is flawed, as are green-cheesed moons
A moon is still great without those who behold
A match must be a match, as a blizzard must bring cold
How grand life would be without the sight of you
At risk of cliché, I want to say…

CHILD

The mind of a child is an amazing thing
Of wonder about wonder it magically brings
A tale of tales that stands on its own
Sans rationale about, pure child only zones
A child takes a toy and breathes life into
A fantasy of joy, a child brings to
A play place, a place that's made up in mind
Of heroes and villains, what a glorious mind
No pennies for thoughts, die Gedanken sind frei
But a nickel for naught is a five cent lie
Of a promise that ought to rid us of why
A future we sought, so unspecified
A child is resilient, so much that it's hard
To believe that they're human, so avant-garde
In thought and behavior, conforming to none
An innocence of mind that life will overrun
And replace with stress and persistent angst
Relationships and money, the epicenter of angst
But memories of thoughts as a child shall remain
Locked in a cage in a bubble in chains
And life will go on for the chosen few
Further separating from a former you
That saw the simplicity in the world, so clear
Adulthood became you, youth never to reappear
Forget it we mustn't, lest we truly lose touch
With dragons and fairies and heroes and such
And worlds of fulfillment, no desires besought
Forget not your youth, pure magic it brought

CHOICES

When maelstrom has struck, duck you must your head beneath
The chances of survival, I must admit are terribly bleak
A nuclear threat approaches and as a mother you must decide
Which life you must save, one minute to decide
Your daughter is your heart, she so reminds you of you
When you were a wee one, so innocent and new
To a world of no remorse and hardship abound
Denying her effectively means you're putting her in the ground
But your son is so dapper, a real gentleman he's become
Do you make his fleeting life susurrus, a dissipating thrum
Or do you choose him to live, over those you also love
It is unfair, but life's not fair, perhaps the Man above
Can guide your decision as you look into your husband's eyes
No tears for you, no love anew, it's time to say goodbye
No forgiveness for a child, but choose him and he's gone
A space for three, but four ye be, to seppuku you are drawn

DENIED LOVE

A million slaves and a thousand blades cannot be denied love
A quintillion moons and a bucket of spoons cannot be denied love
A fourth of a fourth, silly chair on a porch cannot be denied love
A feast for a beast, nature's balance deceased cannot be denied love
A woman on a roof singing songs aloof cannot be denied love
A man in a room slow dancing with a broom cannot be denied love
A country in shambles whilst politicians ramble cannot be denied love
A bride to be in love with her knee cannot be denied love
A watch with no face, gourmet food lacking taste cannot be denied love
A bunny named Dummy that's funny to dummies cannot be denied love
A chasm of hope, life and death eloped cannot be denied love
A person that speaks with silence so deep cannot be denied love
A room with a view of a blossom anew cannot be denied love
A pot in a pan in a pot in one's hand cannot be denied love
A summer of lust, relationships with broken trust cannot be denied love
A sinner reborn to eschew worldly scorn cannot be denied love

DONUT AND COFFEE

If death were a buoy upon which I could cling
A donut and coffee in mind I would bring
I'd bring it for luck and I'd bring it for fear
For fear of the lucky shark that lurks near
I'm trapped in the waters without landfall in sight
No ships to come save me, just cold open nights
No food on my person, just donut in mind
Could swear the shark's smiling with teeth they that grind
A heck of a way to say adieu to the world
Letting loose of death's buoy to be eaten and hurled
With flesh torn apart as my blood gushes out
No air in my lungs, shark's tooth through my mouth
Violence begets violence, so I'd let out a yell
With my last breath, I'd blind it to hell
And plead to dear Hades to let me pass with
My donut and coffee, life's parting gift

DRAGON

If I had a choice in this life or the next
I'd choose to be a dragon
And soar through the skies on silk wings made of lies
What manner, dear boy, of dragon
Has wings made of silk, 'tis as supple as milk
The image gives reason for pause
A dragon is fierce with red eyes, they that pierce
With razor-sharp menacing claws
My dragon is calm, with the world hath no qualms
So, menacing need not it be
My fire is cool, no desire to rule
A nation that does not believe
If magic were magical, dragon sabbatical
Taken to come back to now
As dragon, not man, full of fire and plans
To remedy all that is now
If I had a choice in this life or the next
A dragon I would choose to be
And sit on a rock as I pensively thought
About what it means to be

EGGS AND HAMMY

As babies go gaga and parents go goo goo
As husbands are balding and wives wear their muumuus
But muumuus as jammies with noodles of Bahmi
And New York, a sweet fork of fried eggs and hammy
My hammy, Miami, so hot, no flim flammy
The ramification, elation 'pon Sammy
The reason that treason is prevalent for seasons
Is husbands are balding and God gave no reason
The balding again of the men, oh sweet Christmas
Is here when the cheer borders jeer, that's the litmus
So sing when you see a sincere politician
But wait, it's a dream, so it seems, purely fiction
The fiction of fiction's a mission of diction
The people or power, no clear competition
The world is a stage and we're at our audition
The part is a farce, yet we cling to convictions

FAREWELL

It was not until I saw death that I realized the gift of life
A timer preloaded with breaths, death is so much greater than life
It was not until I saw clouds that I realized the beauty of up
The up, up, and away of a cloud about to bust
And shower me with rain of ancient elements deceased
In Valhalla I shall reign, in death I'll tame the beast
A beast with no name, but fame for its ill will
For will that is ill will fill one's mind until it spills
Death is inevitable, despite accumulated life's wins
How close one gets to heaven is not measured in lack of sins
It's truly hard to imagine that your loved ones will all die
And fade into nothing, leaving memories behind
A mother or a father, a spouse or a child
A relative or friend, from dear life forever exiled
There are no words to abate the pain of lonely dwell
I kiss you on your forehead and bid you farewell

FORGING STEEL

You've got ten seconds and eight of them are gone
So get off my bus or I'll murder you real long
Your mommy and daddy can't save you from this
No mulligans on your choice to raise your right hand and enlist
It's high ho lock and load and shoot, move, communicate
You won't earn a boom boom unless you assimilate
Push-up, sit-up, two-mile run, Sir
When I'm done with you, you'll wish you were dead, Sir
Whirl and whirl, then you fix bayonet
Your lungs fill with dust as you lunge with bayonet
In the chamber of CS, you'll take off that mask
And inhale that evil as I smile and I bask
In the glow of your pain as the old you dies off
And the new you is born, what a sweet payoff
You'll hurt and you'll bleed, but I promise you this
When I'm done forging steel, you'll be a weapon that won't miss

GIVE ME YOUR HAND

Give me your hand, so that I may pull you from your hole
A hole shrouded in doubt, a window needing a soul
A soul needing a window and a rock with which to shatter
The lie of a soul viewed from a window, truth is all that matters
Lightning strikes upon you as plague consumes your thoughts
You contemplate existence, then contemplate the thought
A fireplace of memories and possibilities to be
You smoke your pipe and think of life, the past can never be freed
Give me your hand, so that I may pull you from your hole
I'll yank it high, high five the sky, who gave you such a role
You roll and duck, you bitter schmuck, we love you as you are
You're not on fire, that burn is ire, toward they who tried to bar
The likes of you from that which is true, they know not what they do
The curse of man, a shadowed hand, your world rebuilt anew
I cry my tears, we love you dear, if I could rewind time
I'd save you from that awful crash, I wish I controlled time

GRATEFUL

Don't put off till tomorrow what you can do today
Tomorrow could summon the reaper, who is always a heartbeat away
We find so many reasons to postpone the things we want
Acceptance, love, and happiness is all we truly want
Subservience to the upper caste and being slaves to the job
A groupthink mentality, not far removed from mobs
Normal is acceptable, but should not define your life
Money is a necessity, but should not define your life
You're alive, but not living, as predictable as math
Education, job, and marriage, a preordained path
Nine to five to stay alive, recovery at week's end
You're yet to start living, but the road ahead shall end
Don't wait until it's too late to tell someone you love them
Pursue your dreams and burst those seams and norms ensure you shove them
Out the way and live your days with no regrets or remorse
Be grateful that the fork's ahead, last chance to change your course

GREAT SONG

Like Henry and a hole in the bucket, great song
With what shall he fix it, dear Liza, great song
Solutions that end back at start, great song
Don't save the bucket, fini, great song
Tammy said stand by your man, great song
But what if he's trifling and cheap, great song
And cheating with women, your friends, great song
With your man, you have no friends, great song
Prince, maybe was demanding, great song
Oh doves, how they cried, sweet guitar, great song
A god of a man and a legend, great song
Your rain will always be purple, great song
Yes, Janis was top of her class, great song
Was Bobby McGee the last great song
A piece of my heart that's taken, great song
Get it, she said, while you can, great song
But Barry, a voice so deep, great song
Can't get enough of your love, great song
As Al and Luther gave choice, great song
Between them there is no choice, great song
The Bangles and flames eternal, great song
Bananas and ramas of Venus, great song
Girls just wanna have fun, great song
Blondie and hearts of glass, great song
Gimme a man after midnight, great song
A dancing queen was crowned, great song
By ABBA, but nearby was Michael, great song
Don't stop till you get enough, great song
A wheel in the sky for Journey, great song
A Queen of champions to rock you, great song
Forever and ever, like Rick, great song
I thank you dear artists for such great songs

HOW TO LOSE

If you back the wrong horse and it comes in dead last
Do not disparage the victor, lest they take you to task
If a savvy supercilious foe has bested your best bids
Take it on the chin, but your fury do not rid
Internalize and sit upon it and let it eat your heart
Let it burn your soul and leave your moral compass in parts
Let it stew and come to boil and keep you up at night
A loss should be a motivator to make you want to fight
Fight for land and fight for love and fight for all that's dear
When it reaches fever pitch, your knife into it steer
Shove it deep and scream aloud, as anguish makes you tremble
Madness calls, to knees you fall, a monster you resemble
Escape your cage and summon rage and make it work for you
Destroy the bridge into the moat and take along thumbscrews
For toes to crush and screams to hush, a medley void of ruse
The deal is done, even you've become, this is how to lose

IMMORTALITY

Immortality is worthless without a reason to live
As worthless as a receiver who fails to ever give
In exchange for immortality, you give up your soul
But eternity is lonely, like canaries near coal
You assume new identities and live in strange lands
From England to Sierra Leone to Norway, then Japan
You're Scott, then Morlay, then Bjørn, and Koichiro
Tomorrow's mystery, who you'll be you do not know
You frolic and marry and have many kids
No wills to be read, no patience to be bid
As sure as felled trees in a forest make sound
Someday you'll put your wife and dear children in the ground
With your two hands as the rain falls upon you
You'll wish you were dead as the rain falls upon you
A deal with the gods, how you thought you were clever
Without someone to share life with, what's the point in forever

INSIGNIFICANT

You believe you are important, but in reality you are not
For detritus beneath cover hath equal successful shots
Of achieving something meaningful and living a fulfilled life
This life is but a farce, wrapped in lies, wrapped in strife
We are told that if we succumb and act within confines
We'll have behaved like proper citizenry and not be confined
The rules are for prosperity, everyone can achieve
But if your skin does not look like mine, eventually you'll apperceive
That institutional measures are designed to keep you down
Equality is not equal, you exist in shantytown
The shackles never left you, for the powerful do what they will
The weak can but suffer, such is life below the hill
The humanity of humans has been absent long ago
If your politics differ, my diktat is you are foe
I murder you where you stand, with words or with deeds
I sully your reputation, for your party did not heed
A pity we've all become so cruel to our fellow man
Tribalism is our watchword, obliterate the other clan
Give them no quarter, nor a chance to be represented
We make them mad, then call them mad, and wonder why they are tormented
Love, money, happiness, peace, and all things in between
We seek, but this paradox of a ride is headed to Abilene
Focus on things you can control and enjoy your freedom of thought
At the end of the day, to some dismay, Earth's significance is naught

KETCHUP

Ajar before avatars, that they may walk through to life
Avars and Byzantine, a mere prelude to strife
A conclusion, not illusion, that our characters give way
To traits that according to Dawson, reveal our innermost plays
It is said that a condiment can determine much about
A person through preferences, a most strange readout
As a person that pitches dear quoits on a whim
The chances of escaping ketchup's scry, 'tis but slim
If dunkers are methodical and somewhat in control
Why do sprinklers seek that which makes them whole
Squirters being creative as splodgers calculate
Reveals that smotherers can be the snobs which they hate
The moral of the story is that clairvoyance is all around
From palm and face readers to rumpologists who propound
Their theories about our lives, do we take them at their word
Heed the possibility that in this life all is not absurd

LEARNING AND UNDERSTANDING

I've learned that all life is not valued the same
We are poles in the holes of poles' confusing games
Games that are laced with a trace of androgyny unbridled
Confusion and bemusement at the beauty of fervor unbridled
I've learned that reggae songs at times repeat the first verse
I've learned that life is a script, but as actors, we are poorly rehearsed
A rehearsal for a scene that has played out time and again
You don't look like me, so we can never be friends
You don't speak like me and our religions differ
Your gender is confusing and our political affiliations differ
Your jargon and colloquialisms lead me to believe that you are inferior
I fear what I do not understand, such is the core of my interior
I've learned that people believe that minorities are victims of their own devices
That complaints about the legal system are components of non-factual devices
I've learned that you can't understand a person till you've walked a mile in their shoes
Beset with grief, no worldly relief, to relate means to choose
I've learned that people in movies and commercials do not look like me
Representation is all but non-existent, except tokens meant to appease
I've learned that love is much deeper than a word and at times is overrated
To love someone, to truly love someone, is so powerful it can't accurately be stated
I've learned that death is a mystery to all, it is pain at its finest
Grieving never ends and will consume us all, yes, even the finest
Life and death are not inevitable, all you need is to understand
Hold out your hand and wait for it

Wait for it
Wait for it
Wait for it
I see you still do not understand
Like a tale of a whale with a tail that seemingly had a subtle tell
Not the whale's, though akin, would it serve as a shell
To a view of another whale whose tail intentionally overlapped
To verily shout, to huff and pout, is useless unless you adapt

LEFT AND RIGHT

To the left of your left is my left, this is right
For right of one's left leaves the left left affright
Left makes a choice to become mighty like right
But left can only be left and can never be right
Lest left change composition and orient right of left
Leaving behind all that is definitively left
For death of the left can only give rise
To an imbalance of direction, for only right shall survive
The agony and despair of a world void of left
Casts an ominous shadow leaving one short of breath
With no left left how can one last breath be left
Or a shadow of a dream as it drifts to the left
The right way to leave left leaves left left alone
In a world full of rights right of right in all zones
The trouble with a world full of rights and no lefts
Is when rights die out, there shall be nothing left

LOVE ME NOT

Love me not, not in this world, for I shall break your heart
I am man, a cursed creature, twice removed from the dark
I walk upright and speak coherently a good deal of the time
But fully developed, I cannot envelope, neither with reason, nor rhyme
'Tis a fantasy that you can change me, for man cannot be undone
'Tis mea culpa for all that's faltered, grab your suitcase and run
When you think of me as a loving machine, I wonder what madness
Has taken you, perhaps strange brew, to think man brings gladness
I have brought you war, I have brought you plague and many atrocities in between
I have burned your heroes and killed your prophets, to man, what can love mean
I have made you cry, lied before your eyes and swore till death do us part
Yet taken another to be my young lover, I'm sorry, but I know not my heart
Love me not, for I'll consume you and crush your dreams by mistake
This pavement is slippery, my hands are twitchy, how much abuse must a woman take
Is man worth saving, is faith necessary, a canary in an open cage
A woman bathing in toils of cravings not to be in an open cage
Procreate we must, lest life goes bust and only vestiges remain
There is good in man, but an unfortunate hand, he was dealt beset with chains
The flight of life and the thrill to kill has somehow led to power
I've scorched the earth, an ill-constructed hearth, what more must I devour
For you to see, I'm plain you see, don't see me as complex
I want to change, but all that remains is primal urge and reflex
If I were you and you were me, would you choose to love
Or would you gift this anathema a sweet bouquet of foxgloves

MANIFESTATION OF LOVE

If love manifested, how would it look
Would it have a can in a hand that's not a hand but a hook
Would it make food that's grand yet bland from a book
Would it castle my king with a pawn instead of a rook
If love manifested, would it take me for a drive
And bury my fears in a casket full of lies
Would it label me a landlubber and sing lullabies
Till the lull becomes dull and I slowly close my eyes
If love manifested, would I be smart enough to know
That the quest for something negative is positively zero
As a shell of a sedative is a barrier to mood indigo
I'm a carrier shy of merrier than the inventor of genome
If love manifested, would it give me a high five
Would it tell me I'm a genius, as it gazed into my eyes
Would it tell me I'm an imbecile that shall never be prized
As the square root of life is not life multiplied
If love manifested, would we cease to exist
In our present glory, subservient to our ids
Would we fade into nothingness, scratched off of God's list
Would our disappearance be noticed, would we even be missed
If love manifested, what would it truly mean
Would we all become happy, would all become serene
Would the devil grab a shovel, whistling a happy tune from a scene
Understanding the world is unable to accept such a manifested being

MANKIND

I simply do not like mankind
For they are anything but kind
To those who are different from them
And those who merely seem different to them
What's in it for me, is the question they ask
Internally, before undertaking a task
Is this possibly going to eat up my time
They ask as they impatiently slime
Their way out of commitment or to help another
Be it acquaintance, parent, sister or brother
Half of mankind is completely self-centered
No statistics to support said assessment off-center
But the school of life's lessons has taught me something, thus
When the chips are truly down, present-day man is a bust
I simply do not like mankind
For they are anything but kind
To those who do not worship their god
To those whose professions are not worthy of nods
To those who are old or those who are young
To those who are gay, to former addicts who were strung
To people of color, who are truly not inferior
To the poverty stricken, who are deemed sub-superior
To those with tattoos, which are expressive of their being
To those who are nerds, who omit a void of not being
To single parents that may have gone through divorce
To those subject to inequality, it's all par for the course
I simply do not like mankind
For they are anything but kind
I long to be alone on an island
It may not be much, but it shall be my island

An eagerly awaited manifest-to-be dream
A hammock of leather and triple seams
A house by the ocean with a view, oh so grand
I would leave the world behind with a wave of one hand
With peace of mind and clarity of thought
I'd start a new life with the world as an afterthought
I'd smile at the sun and speak to the moon
I'd read a million books and play a million tunes
Alone and content, I'd remain until the end
When my eyes slowly close and my knees no longer bend
I would look to the stars with a nondescript face
The world is not kind, my transition I'd embrace

MARRIAGE

If love married time, would it give rise to lime
Lime that is bitter, but unlike the filthiness of litter
For litter is a latter of a light load of dirty
Fatter for a fault from a girlfriend that's flirty
If time married reason, would it give rise to treason
Treason that is taken, unbridled angst awakened
Or to sleep for a week to repair besmirched leaks
That are results of quasi-cults and the company one keeps
If reason married seasons, would there be a reason for seasons
Or would the union make seasons stop and give pause for reason
The reason that a season is still a season in the absence of reason
Is that seasons do not require reason to continue being seasons
If love married mangos, would it be sweeter than a tango
A taste that's titillating, whilst countering afterglow abating
For relationships lacking trust, love can be magnanimous
Especially when in competition, for an aisle-walk rendition
Why does a woman marry a man, till this day I don't understand
His benumbed mind is blank, too simple to even give thanks
Too primitive for women's needs, wrapped up in his manly deeds
As stubborn as a bull and chases women and feeds them bull
Why does a man marry a woman, till this day I can't understand
If names are to be foretelling, perhaps, she's a woe unto man
She claims to want true love, but nags like death from above
Constant affirmation required, as flighty as a Barbary dove
Why then should we marry, if love tones may not carry
In winds of predetermined visage, in line with society's image
As Astley stated forever, oh my, that gentleman's clever
Regardless of our destination, as humans, we'll make it together

MEMORY

My memory tried to beguile me into thinking that gaps did not exist
In my recollection of imperfection, my mind redacted my prime list
It's a defense mechanism that protects one's person and the sanctity of being
For pain recalled, mishaps and appall, these are not worth mentally seeing
The loss of a parent, the loss of a child, the loss of a friend perhaps
The loss of a loss, confused and embossed, a victim of memory's trap
A tinker of tales, a catcher of whales, who knows what shall resurface
But did it truly happen, in memorable fashion, what lies beneath the surface
A penny for thoughts, a fortune for naught, seems to be how we pay
For memories abound, though mostly unfound, we recall in our special way
An obol to Charon for ferry work to come, for my mind shall one day die
And leave this world, this truth I know, and need not a clairvoyant to scry
A memory of life, pre-recycled life, from the mighty Chamber of Guf
Omission of needs, but moral reprieve, as life begins with the Guf
Your mind is not real, nor emotions that fill the vessel you know as your being
Life ends in death and death ends in life, so complex the state of being

MESSAGE IN A BOTTLE

You'll wake up one morning and realize you're old
You've worked nine to five, you've worked till you're old
You worked to fund living and lived to fund working
Here's a message in a bottle from past lives lurking
Don't spend another year doing what you don't love
Pursue your dream career, 'cause you're a rightful guv
Money serves a purpose, but valuable it is not
Like bones doused in vinegar on a blood-soaked cot
Living on a prayer is not ideal by any means
Choose the red pill or the blue pill and await your next scene
A scene, not obscene from a daft person's view
But outside of reality, your life is all but through
If you could stuff a message in a bottle to throw in
An ocean or a river or a place that cleanses sin
Would you do it dear and dare you warn the world of what
Becomes of a swing that has withered to a putt

MUSTARD

Her mind told her no, but her heart told her yes
She loves him so much, lest she not forget
In pain and in agony, her bone doth protrude
An eye swollen shut, her stomach void of food
A rib or two cracked, her cheekbone shattered
Hate made him do this, that's all that matters
He says it's her fault that he smacks her around
A boot on her head, face scrapping the ground
A mouth full of blood from having lost two teeth
A dinner plate to the mouth, knocking out two teeth
Bruises on her thigh, strangulation marks on her neck
Clothing ripped to shreds, strewn across the deck
Her mind told her no, but her heart told her yes
No man is worth abuse, this do not forget
You have but one life, why live it in chains
A broken heart will mend, but death forever remains

NATIVE REVERENCE

My love of this life has not worked out as planned
My tears and my strife, blood upon this land
The land of Native Americans, who sacrificed so dear
Yet are regarded with hyphens, unlike those who are near
To power and ideal to what American image means
The right skin tone, no atone in this scene
A scene prima facie, though tribes occupied betimes
They have suffered in riddles and been murdered by rhymes
Cowboys and Indians is how Hollywood portrayed
A feud beyond lewd, between factions, no sway
For conquerors conquer, but usually with code
No women, no children, no fires upon abodes
But life 'tis not fair and codes had they not
Indiscriminate slaughter, even death upon tots
There was blood in the hooves of animals, they that ran
If Squanto were not born, we would have different clans
America would be different, less emphasis on race
As Gwawl was betrayed, so are we as we race
Toward a vision of tolerance and opportunity for all
One smile for success, two smiles for a fall
Tribes deserve more than what they currently possess
Without them no us, give reverence, nothing less
Even Caesar was shocked, "Et tu, Brute?" he said
Take heed who you trust, macabre or not, dead is dead

ONE PERCENT

Create me and I will create you
Show me the meaning of life and I will show you how not to fear death
I will show you heaven and hell within the confines of your belief
But I will show you a universal truth that exists despite religion, if you so choose
There is a world far beyond the stars that is yet to be revealed
A duality of dimension, wherein one exists without existing
A duality of imperceptible prisms, wherein the light of realms is reflected, yet absent
Yet this light is never seen by the naked eye, for we do not understand
We do not understand that we are insignificant
We are simple, we are greedy, we are selfish, we are far from dispassionate
We fight for trivial things and our hearts are blackened with envy and airs of superiority
But there is one percent that is worthy
The one percent that helps those in need and puts others before themselves
The one percent that does the right thing even when no one is looking
The one percent that helps others even though there is nothing to be gained
The one percent that does not seek recognition for their good deeds
This one percent shall collectively inherit all that they behold and beyond
The remaining ninety-nine percent shall only inherit the physical
In part due to their incapability to comprehend the metaphysical
Be one with your mind and seek to evolve
For to evolve is to become that which is part of eternality

ONE WISH

If I had one wish, I'd wish that I had a wish
That would wish away my wish, for a wish should only be a wish
If a wish becomes a wish that can suddenly be used to wish
Then wishes lose their magic, oh my dear that would be so tragic
If I had two wishes, I'd wish for golden stitches
To stitch the wacky well of wishes, leaving no one else with wishes
Wishes that could wish away, our wishless world and make it fray
From wishes that are not for good, I wish I had…I wish I could
If I had three wishes, I'd wish for bottomless ditches
To put the sun and earth and moon into for they condemned Zip Coon
A pauper of a different tune, no drawings for a different rune
A bag of gems and silence loomed, your life condemned whilst in the womb
If I had four wishes, I'd wish that four was one
For four as four is for a lure of three that snuck into the tour
If I switched this wishful wish, then I'd be back at just one wish
And maybe then, this Carrick Bend, would loosen and the cycle end

PARENTS

I often sit and recall my youth
Pondering pensively upon circumstance and truth
As a child, I thought I understood all
And that my guardians were false, for I had evolved
What do parents know of being bullied at school
What do parents know of having to abide by rules
What do parents know of being an outcast and teased
And having a crush on someone that makes your heart bleed
What do parents know of feeling pressure to fit in
What do parents know of teenage emotional whirlwinds
What do parents know of the urge for independence
What do parents know of virtual transcendence
What do parents know of fashion and style
They wear old people clothes that are old people style
What do parents know of going to clubs
They are still dancing jigs and still cutting rugs
What do parents know of youth lingo untold
A lingua franca esoteric to the old
What do parents know of facing tragedy online
When they were little kids, there was no online
Parents don't understand what it's like to be young
They pay bills and raise kids, perhaps heroes unsung
Parents don't understand what it means to want space
Away from the world, to have a hidden face
I often sit and recall my youth
Pondering pensively upon circumstance and truth
As a child I thought I understood all
But my parents were just like me, they simply evolved

PONDER

At times I sit and ponder what the future has in store
Humanity may implode from the greed of life's allure
Lore of tales of wealth and fame and servants they that bid
To do the bidding of the rich, so poverty you rid
Yourself of so you too may glow and have those whom you lead
A void that's void of platitudes, so bloodless blood you bleed
To escalate and elevate your life from simple man
To Übermensch, but worldly stench, remove it not you can
A foe of fiends, but worldly things you cannot come to leave
You tout your faith, but reflect wraiths, of which none shall bereave
For charlatans and artisans, the line may seem so small
As both believe, they've mastered skills that make them not so small
But small in scale, akin to whales that swim the ocean deep
Is what you are, a human scar, enlightenment that seeps
Away from life and still subdues without a presence, yes
Implosion of humanity, a cleansing of duress
For residue of shattered dreams and hopes so unfulfilled
Combine to make a mixture of a potion we shall swill
And mill around and toil away and tinker till we die
A potion we shall swallow and believe our made-up lies
If words could talk and we could not they'd tell us what it means
To offer words of emptiness and burn a bag of memes
If words could talk and we could not, we'd silently just nod
And ponder truth yon side of couth, oh me, oh my, how odd

PURPLE SADNESS

I bid farewell to the Purple One
It split my heart in two
I cried for nights, till the sun shined it's light
It split my heart in two
Prince was a god in a world full of men
That blessed us oh so dear
The last of his kind, legacy left behind
He taught us not to fear
Chasing our dreams, though impossible they seem
To grab ahold and make real
I'd die a thousand deaths and suppress a hundred breaths
If his purple mind I could reveal
For the secret to life, he embodied in life
And succeeded despite many odds
Like Luther and Michael and music-like idols
He transcended cultural nods
And proved to the world that his music was love
With a voice so marvelous to hear
His charm was amazing, guitar trailblazing
Oh, how I wish he were still here
To teach us the secrets of the cherry moon
And purple rain that gently falls
Upon all our lives, how we live in disguise
To win, at first we must fall
A dagger inside my heart as it bleeds
No artist in this life or the next
Can dare to replace, an original, no trace
He gave our hopes context
A life for a life, in this case misdirect
For doves are crying and roam
About as they fly, we look to the sky
The purple angel is now home

RAINBOW (ODE TO SUSAN)

If you were a color in a rainbow
What color would you be
Your loveliness is matched, my dear
By your hopes of what could be
Your dreams and wants and wishes to make
Have suddenly been put on hold
The fate of man and God's sheer hand
Have denied you growing old
The world does not seem fair, my dear
Why should you part so soon
Yet others that are dregs and louts
Parade by a bloody moon
They wreck and wreak such havoc oblique
But are granted continued life
You help and heap a burden so deep
Yet cancer takes your life
If you were a color in a rainbow
What color would you be
Your loveliness is matched, my dear
By what you've grown to be
You gave your friends and family so much
And revealed to me a sacred path
A path for life that smiles at strife
And prompts alternate paths
A wind of change that changes change
You caught me before I could fall
You held such love within your soul
And blessed us with it all
If you were a color in a rainbow
What color would you be
Your loveliness is such, my dear
No color can represent thee

The stars and moon and heavens beyond
Can't rip you from our hearts
You've taught us much, we love you so much
Farewell, your journey now starts

REJECT

If reject were a reject that rejected your call
To reject, yet eject that which you recall
A call from a reject that rejected your stall
And efforts to reject that led to your fall
To recall a reject and moment so strong
Can lead to a reject of logic along
The lines of a reject's perpetual singsong
As pain of rejection burns deep for so long
A reject can't project a project's rejection
Rejection of options leaves options for selection
For options still remain without options, no objection
But alien as alliteration to non-believers, no infection
Complexity of complex, conflation rejected
But confabulate they must, politicians affected
A reject of lust and mediocrity untested
As droves full of rejects reject they that bested
Their best, 'tis not less than the best they could give
Their best, yea it's less than the lives, they that live
To powers that be and the reaper that soars
Above their wracked slumber and grins keeping score
So points for good deeds and a minus for naught
One wishes they could've and should've, yet ought
To own up to fault and remain in direct
Concert with their person, lest become reject

RUN RUN RUN

Run run run, for the game is afoot
Run run run, lest you unknowingly lose a foot
Run run run, for the policewoman cometh
Run run run, why dost thou runneth
Run run run, no one is chasing you
Run run run, have you heard of loose screws
Run run run, vanity in a broken bottle
Run run run, a foot duct-taped to a throttle
Run run run, look high above your head
Run run run, Dionysius' sword may soon make you dead
Run run run, a belief of external conflict
Run run run, a truth of internal conflict
Run run run, for the sun shall soon set
Run run run, your blood the world may let
Run run run, for the wolves shall give chase
Run run run, should you catch the angel that's falling from grace
Run run run, a new world is upon us
Run run run, a simpler world is behind us
Run run run, grab the rope before you drop
Run run run, into an abyss with no stops
Run run run, tell your family you love them
Run run run, place nothing above them
Run run run, from the ashes you must climb
Run run run, and realize you cannot outrun time

SAD HORSE

A kingdom for a horse, but of course, 'tis so mad
A mushroom that looms in the dark, 'tis so sad
But madness for mushrooms in light, oh so weird
Like sadness for horses in flight, by the beard
Of Zeus, so obtuse, wherefore is this so strange
I give you my heart, you give me your strange
Like claymores that say more than "this side go boom"
The sad horse still runs, traipsing over the mushroom
This life is like dice, full of rolls till you die
Each roll full of chance, each chance full of lies
Each lie full of truths, acquiescence be damned
No glitz when you die, no semblance of glam
No waking up tomorrow to see the sad horse still run
No head out the window, cool breeze and warm sun
Can't hide when it's time, sobriquet or a guise
So live your life full, no bloody compromise

SIDES OF A COIN

There are two sides to a coin, so a coin has two sides
I am stating the obvious, but pray patience for this ride
A ride for a patient that does not understand coin physics
Physics of a visit from a patient studying physics
Of coin dynamics and the possibility of discovery
Akin to Monty Python and the quest for shrubbery
A dilly of a dally, such a term of little meaning
A coin in a valley laying flat has no meaning
Except for the valley, whose fate may have been denied
By the opposing side of the coin that does not face the sky
Flip a coin and call it, as it hurls through the air
Anxiety and hope, with bated breath of despair
There are two sides to a coin, so a coin has two sides
The obvious has been stated, yet you continue this ride
A ride that's a quest and a search for definition
Of sorts, dare I snort at coin fate premonition
To think that a coin is adept at prediction
Of outcome to some, dare I vail to submission
And grin as I rise to the eyes of the beholder
A coin is a coin, not a vessel for the beholder
A tool for deciding which way to proceed
A coin is often used to identify who heeds
In sports and in life, a coin flip is the voice
That whispers a lie and promises false choice

TAKE MY BODY HOME

I've lived a life of ups and downs
Take my body home
The Lord my God has watched me drown
Take my body home
Then resurrected me from sin
Take my body home
Change of heart must come from within
Take my body home
To trade in plague for love of Lord
Take my body home
You must accept Him of your own accord
Take my body home
I'm happy knowing that He walks with me
Take my body home
When I leave, please promise me you'll
Take my body home

THE END

Who among you can definitively say
That they understand life after death
With thousands of religions claiming holy books given
They can't all be right about death
Imagine for a moment that life's tender moments
Form the story 'pon which you'll be judged
How your family is treated, good fortune depleted
Be in order lest you be misjudged
By the Lord of the Over, over Lord, please over
Let me in, for I have been good
I've read the Good Book, Book of books about books
I have even turned ashes into wood
We're told that there's choice, so our wants, we do voice
By action or one-way communiqué
He listens, but knows that requests shall unfold
The balance of destiny's say
If He did undo what was planned, thanks to you
The ripple effect would be grand
Neither sea winds, nor oceans or thunderous potions
Are greater than His mighty plan
We say that our faith is what drives our belief
In religions that we hold so dear
Innate, faith is not, rather based on our spots
In the world, wherein which we were reared
Genuflect as you will, but in the end we all die
Despite what religion you cling to
Your faith is your drive, by what will are you alive
The pendulum does not always swing true
Your family is great and your colleagues are great
You seem to not be on your own
That's what you've been taught, but that lecture was for naught
For everybody dies alone

THE MOON AND BEYOND

Before flying to the moon and leaving me there
Pump out my lungs and suck in the air
Trim the toenails on nine of my toes
Then wiggle the tenth and break it with oh
What have you done, the toe is now blue
I need a Band-Aid or bottle of glue
Here I am, here I am, ready to mend
Oh shucks, oh shoot, you've done it again
Oh me, oh my, here's mud in my eye
We should be more cautious, I cannot deny
The idea of ships to the moon is a blast
Gas up that rocket and gas it up fast
I'll laugh when I get there and smile at the sun
I'll pray to the moon as I basically run
Away from the earth, sweet planet despair
I want to say yay, but I've run out of air

THE WORLD IS NOT BIG ENOUGH

The world is not big enough for all to coexist
And all believe their Savior has selected them for His list
A list that is special, filled with believers and the few
Who devote themselves to gospel and earthly science eschew
The world may not be big enough, but possesses a magnificent core
But a core upon a plague upon a core is neither nor
Nor not a knot in a core that is basal at its best
A core without stability is like a hero lacking a quest
The world is not big enough for all to coexist
Hath your Savior non-believers on His ultra-lengthy list
A list that is special for its content and its matter
A key into the hole of the illusive ever after
After ever after, do the poor and rich sit down
Do vagabonds and cops share upside down frowns
An after that comes after sheer brutality of man
Where power rules corruptly and enslaves a fellow man
The world is not big enough for all to coexist
Some would tiptoe on a graveyard if it meant they'd make the list
Some would put you in a graveyard, minus one name on the list
Our cruelty to others, truly something must be amiss
Amassing of schadenfreude feelings of contempt
For others who excel, pure ire dost thou tempt
A crayon with no color and off-center center-left
Leaves crayons that have color with opacities of death
The world is not big enough for all to coexist
I plead thee elbowroom, three feet my dear, I must insist
And since I am insisting, dare I make one last request
I'd love to have a love for love and live a life of zest
But room I have not here, no no, the world is just too small
Tectonic plates and drift come back, we need to cleanse it all
From death of love or love of death, we cherish not mankind
The world will not be big enough until altruism we find

TIME MACHINE

If I had a time machine
I'd hop in and go for a ride
I'd ride it for fun, as adrenaline is spun
Challenged by death and its guise
A gaggle of geese on the ground
As a skein takes flight in the air
Circling low, as my time machine flows
In their stream with my lungs lacking air
A being that is dead in one time
Yet, living in parallel lines
Awaiting a sign that the death of mankind
Erases the death in his mind
A machine that can travel in time
Perpetrating chronological mime
Would allow for detour, as I sneak through the door
Saving lemons and murdering limes

TWIST

A revolution of sorts that begets a fourth
Of cyanide ramblings besmirched by ramblings
A pinnacle of parley surpassed by hearsay
Say you hear a bypass, Sir, backwards was the latter half, Sir
A neophyte enthralled by nothing at all
For she has to learn that to learn she must learn
As a coat on a hanger has no qualms with said hanger
A hanger of anger that does not hang is still a hanger
Some bread with some cheese, a pregnant woman at ease
Like a smoker under hypnosis, like the phenomenon of apoptosis
I ramble because I gamble on a gimbal that's far from nimble
Like the silence and the sound by dear Simon, so profound
As a ripple tortures tickle, taking turns toward fickle
Loyalty, 'tis but a word, let me tell you what's absurd
What's absurd is the way that real reason brings dismay
May this bring a reason real, lesson's over, stop the reel

WHEN I'M OLD

When I'm old and feeble to boot
What frame of mind will I be in
I once marked time, now I'm losing time
I'm withering to my chagrin
When I'm old and feeble to boot
Who shall care for me
Will children abandon and leave me abandoned
I hope it shan't come to be
I can't recall if I was appalled
At hearing what happened to those
Who grew old and thought, about life, how they fought
Why did life tilt up its nose
And leave them alone, like a dog with a bone
That lacks teeth with which to gnaw
This life is aloof or to the dog it's awoof
Either way, the story is flawed
For people should be, around those, they that love
Not subject to lonely respite
When you give your all, on your sword, you dare fall
Twice dead in a single life
When I'm old and feeble to boot
Just lay me down to rest
I hate to say bye, but my well has run dry
Passage, the ultimate test

WHERE YOU STAND

Consider for a brief moment that the earth is not round
That the floor is the ceiling and the ceiling is the ground
That your husband is your jailer and you can no longer speak
That the wicked inherit the earth as they set on fire the meek
If water were replaced with evil and wine
As bosoms of deceit and carnage unwind
Would wives as jailers preemptively seize sight
No more staring at other women, no more long kisses goodnight
What if blood ran cold as it touched hot stone
What if all men disappeared, would women bemoan
A killing without billing or conviction to boot
The filling of coffers with imaginary loot
When meanies become nice and the sun turns to ice
When whiskey is our topping for a bland bowl of rice
When horses run wild across cyan-colored tears
You'll know where you stand, but not what you fear

www.ingramcontent.com/pod-product-compliance
Lightning Source LLC
Chambersburg PA
CBHW030134100526
44591CB00009B/647